DRAW WHAT YOU SEE

The Life and Art of Benny Andrews

by Kathleen Benson

Illustrated with paintings by Benny Andrews

Clarion Books
Houghton Mifflin Harcourt
Boston New York

Clarion Books
215 Park Avenue South
New York, New York 10003

Clarion Books is an imprint of Houghton Mifflin Harcourt Publishing Company.

www.hmhco.com

The illustrations in this book are original works by Benny Andrews.
The text was set in Bryant Regular.

Library of Congress Cataloging-in-Publication Data
Benson, Kathleen, author.
Draw what you see : the life and art of Benny Andrews / by Kathleen Benson ; illustrated with paintings
by Benny Andrews.
pages cm
ISBN 978-0-544-10487-7 (hardcover)
1. Andrews, Benny, 1930–2006—Juvenile literature. 2. Artists—United States—Biography—Juvenile
literature. 3. African American artists—Biography—Juvenile literature. I. Andrews, Benny, 1930–2006,
illustrator. II. Andrews, Benny, 1930–2006. Works. Selections. III. Title.
N6537.A52B46 2015
759.13—dc23   [B]   2013046203

Manufactured in China
SCP 10 9 8 7 6 5 4 3 2 1
4500493849

In memory of Jim Haskins

I am grateful to Janice Shay of Pinafore Press for envisioning this book and for making it possible for me to meet Benny Andrews. Special thanks to Nene Humphrey, Benny's widow, for her helpful suggestions, and to halley k. harrisburg of the Michael Rosenfeld Gallery for hers. Finally, kudos to Lynne Polvino for a superb editing job.

—K.B.

NEW ORLEANS, LOUISIANA
2005

When Hurricane Katrina hit New Orleans, whole families lost their homes. People had to live in camps set up by the government or move miles away to stay with relatives or friends. Children had to go to makeshift schools.

The artist Benny Andrews traveled from New York City to Louisiana to work with those children. He showed them how to draw pictures of what they had seen, to use art to express their feelings about what they had been through. He knew from his own experience how important this kind of self-expression was. And he knew that sometimes it was easier to tell a story with pictures than with words.

Plainview, Georgia
1933

Benny started to draw when he was three years old. Once he started, he never stopped.

At first, he made pictures of the world around him. He drew hot suns and red clay and little wood-frame houses in the middle of cotton fields that stretched as far as he could see. He drew black people at work in the fields.

Just about everyone Benny knew worked in the cotton fields, on farms owned by white people. Every morning except Sunday, they reported to white bosses. Benny's mama and daddy had other jobs, too. They had ten children to feed.

On Sundays, the family went to church. Benny loved the colorful hats the women wore. He sang hymns at the top of his voice, swaying with the congregation. When the preacher shouted about suffering and justice, Benny made pictures in his mind. Back home, he drew the church ladies' hats and the preacher's Bible stories.

In grade school, Benny was always the class artist. He copied the comics from the daily newspaper. He drew the stories he heard on the radio and the stars in the movies he went to see in town on Saturdays.

After school, Benny worked carrying water to the laborers in the fields. At planting and harvest time, he didn't go to school at all. None of the black children in Plainview did, because they were needed on the farms. Their school year was only about five months long.

By the time they were teenagers, most of Benny's friends went to work in the fields full-time. But Benny was miserable there. Every row of crops was the same as every other row. The hot sun beat down through the straw hat on his head. The hoe was heavy in his hands.

Benny dreamed of leaving. He did not have a clear plan, but he knew the first step was to attend high school. He was glad when his mother made arrangements with their farm's boss, Mr. Will, so he could go.

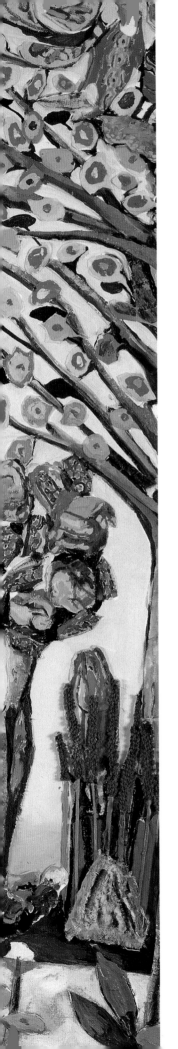

Each day, Benny had to walk three miles to high school and then three miles back home. But he knew that there was a bigger world waiting for him beyond the small world of his childhood, and that getting an education was the best way to reach it. He wanted to see that world for himself and make pictures of it.

Benny graduated from high school, and with a scholarship from the local 4-H Club, he went to a small college for black students. Then he joined the air force, and finally got a chance to travel. The air force sent him all over the United States, even to Alaska. During all that time, he never stopped drawing.

When Benny's military service was over, the government offered to pay his college tuition. He moved to Chicago to attend art school. It was the biggest city he had ever seen, full of many different kinds of people, towering buildings, and—best of all—museums. Benny could spend an entire day looking at art if he wanted. He'd never felt so free.

Home was always in his heart. But Plainview, Georgia, and the white bosses, and the black farm workers, and the rows of crops, all the same, were far behind him now.

Benny was inspired by the people around him, and people were what he wanted to draw. He especially liked making paintings of the jazz musicians in the city's many clubs and cafés. He loved meeting them and listening to their music, and he learned how to show the rhythms of their songs in his artwork. With lots of practice, he became a master at capturing movement on the still canvas.

Benny also made pictures of the ordinary people he saw, like the janitors who worked at his school. He liked to think of himself as a "people's painter." And he discovered that sticking pieces of paper and canvas on his pictures made them seem more textured and real.

After art school, Benny moved to New York City and became a working artist. He had so many stories to tell. He began to create a series of paintings about his childhood in Georgia. Making several pictures based on the same theme was a whole new way for him to tell stories with his artwork. He painted the people on the streets of Harlem, the happiness and sadness that he saw, and the demonstrations that marked the beginnings of the civil rights movement.

Benny fought for equal rights for African Americans—especially artists. He protested against museums and galleries that did not exhibit the work of women and people of color. He formed a group that helped organize exhibitions of artwork by those who were often excluded by the art world.

Benny also began to teach, first at a community center, and then at a college. He took his students to a prison to teach art to the inmates. He believed that art was for everyone.

Benny Andrews worked hard his entire life. And all that work paid off—he became a respected artist. His paintings were shown at big museums, art galleries, community centers, and colleges. He made pictures for children's books.

Benny's success made him even more determined to help others, and to share his love of art with them. He continued to teach people from many different backgrounds to use art to tell their stories—and to start, as he did, by drawing what they see.

Benny Andrews, 2003. Photograph by Chia Chong.

More About Benny Andrews

Born in 1930 in Plainview, Georgia, Benny Andrews grew up in a time and place when African Americans were not supposed to dream. But he had big dreams. He was not supposed to get an education beyond grade school, yet he graduated from high school and college. His dreams took him far from the farm where his parents were sharecroppers, but he never forgot where he came from. The segregation and poverty of his childhood informed both his life and his art.

When the civil rights movement began to bring change to the United States, particularly in the South, he returned home to see for himself what those changes meant for black people. Many years later, he was honored by his home state with awards and museum exhibitions of his work. He could have refused, bitter over his childhood suffering; instead, he graciously accepted this belated welcome home.

Benny Andrews fought hard to change the art world by protesting the exclusion of women and artists of color from museum and gallery collections and exhibitions. As visual arts director of the National Endowment for the Arts in Washington, D.C., from 1982 to 1984, he worked to establish a health insurance program and opened doors for many underrepresented artists.

When most American artists were painting abstract forms, he chose to paint realistic, figural ones. He celebrated his own life and the lives of ordinary people, capturing their images on canvas. He became a teacher both inside and outside the classroom, encouraging students, prisoners, fellow artists, and children who had experienced tragedy to take ownership of their stories by drawing, painting, and writing about them. He was a "people person," and even when he became famous, he always had time for others.

Sources and Resources

Benny Andrews: The Bicentennial Series. Exhibition Catalog. Atlanta, GA: The High Museum of Art, 1975.

Benny Andrews: There Must Be a Heaven. Exhibition Catalog. New York: Michael Rosenfeld Gallery, 2013.

Benny Andrews: The Visible Man. Video. L&S Video, Inc., 1996.

The Collages of Benny Andrews. Exhibition Catalog. New York: Studio Museum in Harlem, 1988.

Gruber, J. Richard. *American Icons: From Madison to Manhattan, the Art of Benny Andrews, 1948–1997.* Jackson, MS: University Press of Mississippi, 2005.

Timeline: The Life of Benny Andrews

1930 Born November 13 in Plainview, near Madison, Georgia

1933 Makes his first drawings

1935 Enters Plainview Elementary School

1944 Enrolls in Burney Street High School in Madison, three miles away

1948 Graduates from high school; enrolls at the all-black Fort Valley State College on a partial scholarship from the 4-H Club

1950 Enlists in the United States Air Force

1954 Is honorably discharged from the USAF, takes advantage of the GI Bill to enroll in the School of the Art Institute of Chicago, where he is one of only a handful of black students

1958 Earns his bachelor of fine arts degree; moves to New York City

1959 Marries Mary Ellen Jones Smith, with whom he has three children

1960 First solo exhibition at the Kessler Gallery in Provincetown, Massachusetts

1964 The Forum Gallery mounts a solo exhibition of his paintings, and his artwork is shown at the New York World's Fair

1965 With funding from the John Hay Whitney Foundation, returns to rural Georgia to reconnect with his family and to see the impact of the civil rights movement on the place where he grew up; creates a group of works titled *The Autobiographical Series*

1966 Begins a long career teaching drawing and painting classes at colleges and community centers

1967 *The Autobiographical Series* is exhibited throughout New York City under the auspices of Union Settlement Association in East Harlem, New York

1968 Creates first book illustrations for *I Am the Darker Brother*, a poetry anthology edited by Arnold Adoff; begins teaching at Queens College, New York

1969 Is elected one of three co-chairs of the Black Emergency Cultural Coalition (BECC); organizes protests against major New York museums that discriminate against artists of color

1972 Establishes a prison-college seminar that takes Queens College students into New York City detention centers to teach art

1973 Receives a fellowship to spend the summer at the MacDowell Colony in Peterborough, New Hampshire; the City of New York honors him for his work in the prison system

1974 Documentary film *The 24-Hour a Day Life of Benny Andrews* is produced; he accepts a position as a visiting critic at Yale University, is awarded a National Endowment for the Arts grant, and receives a second MacDowell fellowship

1976 Pickets the Whitney Museum of American Art's exhibition 300 Years of American Art, which includes no black artists and only one (white) woman; serves as guest curator of an exhibition of artwork by prisoners at the Studio Museum in Harlem; joins the MacDowell Fellows Committee and the advisory board of the National Center of Afro-American Artists

1980 Creates a 95-foot-long mural, *Flight*, for the Hartsfield-Jackson Atlanta International Airport in Georgia

1982 Is appointed visual arts director for the National Endowment for the Arts (NEA) in Washington, D.C.; serves for two years

1983 At the NEA, initiates a project to provide health insurance for people working in the arts; donates all his archival material to the Studio Museum in Harlem

1985   Is honored by the National Council of Arts Administrators for "making a major contribution to the arts in America"

1986   Marries artist Nene Humphrey

1987   Is named the first distinguished Martin Luther King Jr.–César Chávez–Rosa Parks Visiting Professor at the University of Michigan; named to the board of the MacDowell Colony

1990   First overseas one-man show opens at the Overholland Museum in Amsterdam, The Netherlands

1992   Is honored by the Georgia State Council on the Arts for his contributions to the arts

1993   Is honored as Artist of the Year by the Studio Museum in Harlem

1995   The retrospective exhibition Benny Andrews: Thirty-Five Years opens at the Afro-American Cultural Center at North Carolina State College, Raleigh

1996   *Benny Andrews: The Visible Man,* a film documentary, is released

1997   Is elected to membership in the National Academy of Design, New York City; *American Icons: From Madison to Manhattan, the Art of Benny Andrews, 1948–1997,* is published

1999   The exhibition Benny Andrews: A Different Drummer opens at the American Jazz Museum in Kansas City, Missouri; Benny Andrews and Nene Humphrey receive artist-in-residence fellowships at the Hambridge Center in northern Georgia

2000   The Art of Family, an exhibition of work by Benny Andrews and Nene Humphrey, opens at the High Museum of Art in Atlanta

2005   After Hurricane Katrina forces thousands of New Orleans residents to scatter, travels to Louisiana to encourage the children who survived the storm to draw and paint their experiences

2006   Dies of cancer at his home in New York; first posthumous exhibition, The John Lewis Series of collages, created to illustrate the children's book *John Lewis in the Lead: A Story of the Civil Rights Movement,* opens at the Parish Gallery, Washington, D.C.

2007   The Andrews Humphrey Family Gallery at the Ogden Museum of Southern Art, University of New Orleans, is established

2008   In August, the Benny Andrews Foundation donates more than 300 of Andrews's artworks to the United Negro College Fund (UNCF), which will distribute these works to appropriate cultural and educational institutions, with the purpose of using them as the foundation for arts education initiatives such as lectures, workshops, and similar programming

2012   *Portrait of the Black Madonna* (1987) by Andrews is featured on the cover of the catalog for African American Art: Harlem Renaissance, Civil Rights Era, and Beyond, a traveling exhibition organized by the Smithsonian American Art Museum

2013   Michael Rosenfeld Gallery presents Benny Andrews: There Must Be a Heaven, the first comprehensive retrospective since the artist's death, accompanied by a fully illustrated color catalog with an essay by Dr. Lowery Stokes Sims

2014   In observance of the fiftieth anniversary of the Civil Rights Act of 1964, the Brooklyn Museum presents the group exhibition Witness: Art and Civil Rights in the Sixties, highlighting *Witness* (1968) by Andrews on its catalog cover

MORE ABOUT THE ART

Front jacket: *Umbrellas* (America Series). Oil and collage on paper. 1990.

p. 4: *Cotton Monument* (Interior Series). Oil on joined paper with painted fabric and paper collage. 2002.

p. 7: *The Soil* (America Series). Oil on paper with painted fabric collage. 1990.

p. 8: *Down the Road.* Oil on canvas with painted fabric collage. 1971.

p. 11: *Black Church* (Langston Hughes Series). Oil on three sheets of joined paper with painted fabric collage. 1996.

p. 12: *Corner Greeters* (Migrant Series). Oil and collage on paper. 2004.

p. 15: *Writing to Dr. Martin Luther King.* Oil and collage on paper. 2005.

pp. 16–17: *The Promised Land* (Migrant Series). Oil and collage on canvas. 2004.

p. 19: *Reception Study #11* (Interior Series). Oil and collage on paper. 2002.

pp. 20–21: *The Cotton Club* (Migrant Series). Oil and fabric collage on canvas. 2004.

pp. 22–23: *Harlem USA* (Migrant Series). Oil and collage on canvas. 2004.

p. 25: *Free Spirits* (Human Spirit Series). Oil and collage on paper. 2000.

p. 26: *The Reception* (Interior Series). Oil and collage on canvas. 2002.

Back jacket: *Migration Blues* (Musical Interlude Series). Oil and collage on paper. 1998.

All images appear courtesy of the Benny Andrews Estate and Michael Rosenfeld Gallery LLC, New York, NY, with the exception of the photograph on p. 28, which appears courtesy of Savannah College of Art and Design, the Benny Andrews Estate, and Michael Rosenfeld Gallery LLC, New York, NY.

Benny Andrews working on the Migrant Series in his Brooklyn, New York, studio, 2004.